Zoffany and his Tribuna

STUDIES IN BRITISH ART

Zoffany
and his Tribuna

OLIVER MILLAR

The Paul Mellon Foundation for British Art 1966
London Routledge & Kegan Paul

First published in Great Britain 1967
By The Paul Mellon Foundation for British Art, 38 Bury Street,
London, S.W.1. in association with Routledge & Kegan Paul
Ltd., Broadway House, Carter Lane, London, E.C.4

The Paul Mellon Foundation for British Art (a Charitable Trust registered under the Charities Act 1960) was established in 1962 at the initiative of Mr Paul Mellon. Its purpose is to advance the study of British painting, sculpture and the graphic arts mainly by its sponsorship of publications and its support of art-historical research.

Library of Congress catalogue card no. 67–16159
Printed in Great Britain by Westerham Press, Westerham, Kent
Designed in the offices of The Paul Mellon
Foundation for British Art

Plates

Acknowledgments

The following have kindly given permission for works in their possession to be reproduced

Bayerische Staatsgemäldesammlungen, Munich 9
The Viscountess Gage 12
The late Mr Donald Hyde 27
Kunsthistoriches Museum, Vienna 26
Metropolitan Museum of Art, New York 8, 35
National Portrait Gallery, London 2
Palazzo della Pilotta, Parma 33, 34
Uffizi Gallery, Florence 17, 18, 19, 32
Mrs Mary van Berg, New York 10

Photographic Acknowledgments

Thos. Agnew & Sons Ltd 27
Alinari/Mansell Collection 32
A. C. Cooper Ltd 3–6, 13–15, 20, 21, 23, 24, 28
Royal Academy of Arts 12, 25
Mr John D. Schiff, New York 10
University of London, Courtauld Institute 16, 22, 29, 30
Comm. Vaghi, Parma 33, 34

Plate 1 Benedetto de Greyss *View of the Interior of the Uffizi*
Gabinetto dei Disegni, Uffizi, Florence

Foreword

When I began to draft an entry for Zoffany's *Tribuna of the Uffizi* for inclusion in the Catalogue of the Later Georgian Pictures in the royal collection, it soon became apparent that it was possible to collect far too much material for that particular context. The story, which is a good one, was therefore put together in the form of a Lecture given at the Courtauld Institute on 1 December 1964. The generosity of the Paul Mellon Foundation has made it possible to print and illustrate the Lecture. I have amplified some of the quotations and in fairly copious footnotes I have provided references and additional information; in two Appendixes I have printed Farington's unpublished notes on Zoffany's career and certain documents relating to his work on the picture. But I have kept for the main body of the text the form in which the Lecture was delivered.

The picture itself is reproduced, and the extracts from Farington's MSS. are printed, by gracious permission of Her Majesty The Queen.

The documents in the Archivio degli Uffizi are printed by kind permission of the Soprintendenza of the Gallery. I would like to record my gratitude to Dottoressa Luisa Becherucci and Dottoressa Giulia Sinibaldi in the Uffizi, to Signora Anna Maria Ciaranfi Francini at the Pitti and to Miss Anna Maria Crinò for their help in collecting material in Florence. I am equally grateful to Professor Ulrich Middeldorf and Dr. Detlef Heikamp. Mr. Warren H. Smith, Associate Editor of the Yale Edition of Horace Walpole's Correspondence, most kindly provided me with accurate transcripts of Sir Horace Mann's letters to Walpole; and Mr. Brinsley Ford was infinitely generous in making available to me his information on the movements and activities of Englishmen in Italy.

1 January, 1965   O.N.M.

1 I have based this brief account of Zoffany's early years on Farington's unpublished biographical notes on Zoffany which are printed in Appendix A: notes based on information from the painter himself in 1795, his widow in 1811, and one of his pupils in 1804; the facts in them are sometimes at variance. The years of Zoffany's career that are covered in this Lecture occupy the first three chapters of the biography of the artist (1922) by Lady Victoria Manners and G. C. Williamson.

2 A little-known portrait, painted early in Zoffany's first London period, is of Richard Neville Neville at Audley End; Zoffany was paid £6 for this on 5 November 1761 (R. J. B. Walker, *Audley End . . . Catalogue of the Pictures in the State Rooms*, 3rd ed. (1964), p.45). It seems to be close in style to Benjamin Wilson. More puzzling is a portrait in the possession of Sir Arundell Neave. This is signed by Zoffany and bears a later inscription with the date 1751. It seems inconceivable that this could have been painted before Zoffany arrived in England (Arts Council, *Johann Zoffany*, 1960-1 (1)).

3 J. Watkins, *Memoirs of . . . Sophia-Charlotte, Queen of Great Britain* (1819), p.178. In 1771, indeed, Zoffany himself was said to be going to Italy to buy pictures for the king (H. Walpole, *Anecdotes of Painting in England* (1760-95), ed. F. W. Hilles and P. B. Daghlian, vol. V (Yale Univ. Press 1937), p.83.

4 I am grateful to Mr. Geoffrey de Bellaigue and Mr. John Harris for their help in identifying the items in this and the following pictures.

The year 1772 marks a watershed in the career of Zoffany. He was thirty-eight years of age (he had been born near Frankfurt am Main on 13 March 1734 of a German mother and an Hungarian father) and, twelve years before, he had come to England. Twenty-two years earlier, in 1750, he had run away from his apprenticeship and friends to embark on an enthusiastic journey to Italy, part of which he is said to have made on foot. In Italy he studied for seven years under Agostino Massucci and Mengs; on his return he was for three years in the service of the Elector of Treves; and in 1760 he came to England.[1]

At first he worked as a drapery painter for Benjamin Wilson. They parted after a quarrel, but Zoffany was fast building up a reputation as a painter of conversation-pieces and small full-length portraits; from this period dates the *Self-portrait* [Plate 2] in the National Portrait Gallery. David Garrick became an admirer of Zoffany and took him under his wing. The actor sat to Zoffany 'in various characters' and encouraged him to develop his genius for painting theatrical scenes. In 1762 Zoffany scored an immediate success when he exhibited at the Society of Artists his picture of Garrick in *The Farmer's Return from London*.[2] Among those who admired the picture was Lord Bute, who introduced him to the royal family. Within a short time Zoffany was painting for the young king, George III, and his German consort, Charlotte of Mecklenburg-Strelitz, charming domestic scenes which tell us incidentally something of the appearance of the interior of Buckingham House. This was now the new king's principal residence. During the 1760's it was enriched with a superb library, English furniture and some of the finest pictures brought from the other royal palaces. Further, 'large commissions were sent to Italy for the purchase of paintings, antiques, and other curious articles, to enrich this favourite mansion'.[3] In these enlightened activities the king was following, with the encouragement of Lord Bute, the example of his father, Frederick, Prince of Wales, and not that of George II, his grandfather and predecessor on the throne.

Perhaps the earliest of the royal conversation-pieces that survive in the royal collection is the picture [Plate 3] of the Second Drawing-room or Warm Room at Buckingham House, with two little princes playing with a dog in the foreground; they are probably the king's two eldest sons, George and Frederick. Every detail of this elegant apartment is set before us, the plain English furniture, the marble fireplace (which survives at Windsor), the pretty rococo overmantel in which is reflected a door-case designed by the king himself, and the paintings: two well-known groups by Van Dyck, Maratti's *Infant Christ* and portraits of the princes' parents.[4] Zoffany was developing his peculiar talent for the meticulously accurate rendering of furniture and works of art in their actual setting; but he may, significantly, have slightly falsified the disposition of the pictures in order to make a point

Plate 2 Johann Zoffany *Self-Portrait* Oil on canvas $20\frac{3}{4} \times 16\frac{1}{4}$ inches
National Portrait Gallery London

Plate 3 Johann Zoffany *Prince George and Prince Frederick in an interior in Buckingham House*
Oil on canvas 44 × 50⅜ inches Reproduced by gracious permission of
Her Majesty the Queen

Plate 4 Johann Zoffany *Queen Charlotte at her Dressing-Table, with Prince George and Prince Frederick* Oil on canvas 44¼ × 50⅞ inches Reproduced by gracious permission of Her Majesty the Queen

or suggest a sentiment: there is no evidence that the Maratti was ever in the Warm Room and it is placed over two royal portraits (which do not survive in the royal collection and may, indeed, have been concocted by Zoffany) as if to bless the king and queen and their issue.

In the picture [Plate 4] in which Zoffany paints the young queen interrupted in her toilet by her two eldest sons in fancy dress, the group is more successfully composed and more happily related to the design as a whole than are the two diminutive figures in the Warm Room. The fine objects in the Queen's Dressing-room are suggested more subtly; and there is, in the reflection of this room in a big wall-mirror between the windows and in the glimpse through the doorway of other rooms on the garden front of Buckingham House, a valuable and tantalising glimpse of how the new pictures from Consul Smith's collection – the Canalettos and Zuccarellis for instance – were arranged, hanging close together in their pretty Venetian frames.

In 1772 Zoffany painted the portrait [Plate 5] of the old optician and lens-maker John Cuff, seated at his bench with an assistant at his elbow. It had either been commissioned by the king and queen or was purchased by them soon after it was painted,[1] but it is, as a sympathetic portrait of a craftsman, and of the tools that surrounded him at work, in a very different mood from Zoffany's royal groups.

In 1769 Zoffany had received the peculiar honour of nomination by the King, as opposed to election, to the new Royal Academy, and in 1772 he exhibited there his *Portraits of the Academicians of the Royal Academy* [Plate 6]. This shows his skill, on a more extensive scale, in assembling a large number of figures and in giving to the design as a whole, and to

[1] In the inventory of pictures at Kew *temp.* George III the sitter is described as 'Mr. Cuff – Optician'; a more fanciful title, *The Lapidaries*, first appears in Redgrave's inventory (1859) and the sitter was later identified as Peter Dollond who was, however, only forty-two in 1772.

Plate 6 Johann Zoffany *The Academicians of the Royal Academy* Oil on canvas
$39\frac{3}{4} \times 58$ inches Reproduced by gracious permission of Her Majesty the Queen

Plate 5 Johann Zoffany *John Cuff with an Assistant* Oil on canvas
$35\frac{1}{4} \times 27\frac{1}{4}$ inches Reproduced by gracious permission of Her Majesty the Queen

the individual groups, the true conversation air, and his assurance in working direct on to the canvas, even where intricate detail was to be painted. 'He made no design for it', wrote Walpole in his catalogue of the exhibition – and it is significant that no preliminary drawings survive for any of the pictures by Zoffany that are discussed in this Lecture – 'but clapped in the artists as they came to him, and yet all the attitudes are easy and natural, most of the likenesses strong'. There is no doubt that Zoffany could admirably catch a likeness. Even though Walpole had thought his portrait of George III, shown at the Royal Academy in 1771, 'most disagreeable and unmeaning', he had to confess that it was also 'very like'.

Zoffany had by now come in contact with Joseph Banks who had sailed to the South Pacific with Cook in 1768. In Banks's eyes, the essential ability in an artist was that he could draw animals and plants with accuracy and scientific detachment. The painters he admired most were Paul Potter, Paul Sandby, Wright of Derby, Stubbs and Zoffany. He had, on the other hand, no sympathy with the classical ideals so ardently enshrined in Reynolds's *Discourses*; what mattered to him was that the Patagonian penguin should be induced to sit for his portrait. As for the Grand Tour, Banks contemptuously dismissed it: 'Every blockhead does that'. But even the anti-classical Banks found himself writing of the women of Tahiti: 'Such the Grecians were from whose model the Venus of Medicis was copied'. When, on 28 November 1771, Cook was put in command of a second expedition, to determine the existence of the Southern Continent, Banks enthusiastically joined the project. He formed a team of artists to go with him – Daniel Solander, John Cleveley and Zoffany – but found that the accommodation available on board for his artists and their equipment was inadequate. In May 1772 he withdrew from the expedition.[1]

Zoffany was now high and dry and probably in a restless and unsettled state. He suffered, in any case, from a 'congenital incontinence of the purse';[2] and he had, in Farington's words 'given up his house & business,[3] and displeased many of his patrons by leaving their pictures in an unfinished state'. He made up his mind to return to Italy. Queen Charlotte, when he told her of his plan, 'patronised Him, and procured him letters of introduction to the principal persons there, with a present of £300 for His Journey, and an order to paint for Her, the Florence Gallery'. This was indeed a turning point in Zoffany's career. It is intriguing to consider that only the height of a cabin roof on board the *Resolution* had diverted Zoffany from the excitement of seeing the landscape, inhabitants, culture and flora of the Southern Seas. From the stimulus of civilisations radically different from those in which the arts of the West were grounded, Zoffany turned away from such a challenge, back to the ideals which he had absorbed in his youth in Italy, and set out to paint a picture, which epitomised those ideals, in a city that Ozias Humphry described as 'that most beautiful of cities, the cradle of our art'.[4] The Patagonian penguin was, in other words, abandoned in favour of Sir Horace Mann and the *Madonna della Sedia*: a wiser course, so Walpole thought, than 'his going to draw naked savages, and be scalped with that madman Banks'.[5]

The Grand Duke of Tuscany's collection was generally regarded as the finest in Europe and, although neither Queen Charlotte nor the king had ever seen it, it is not surprising that she should have wished to know what it really looked like, especially as she and the king were so actively engaged at this time in arranging their own pictures around them. And although the king had not been to Italy, two of his younger brothers, the Dukes of York and Gloucester, had travelled there. The Duke of York had made a Grand Tour in 1764, when he had sat in Rome to Batoni, played the leading part in a caricature group by Patch in Florence, and been painted with a group of his friends and members of his household by Brompton in Padua. The Duke of Gloucester, compelled to travel abroad by his injudicious marriage, spent much time in Italy. Apart from the reports of her brothers-in-

1 The Banks episode, and its implications, are discussed by B. Smith, *European Vision and the South Pacific* (1960).

2 W. Hazlitt, *Conversations of James Northcote, Esq, R.A., Collected Works*, ed A. R. Waller and A. Glover, vol. VI (1903), p.386.

3 On 17-18 August 1772 Christie's sold the contents of Zoffany's house, garden and stables at his dwelling situated near the Six Mile Stone on the road leading to Brentford: garden tools, wine, plate, a high-bred bay gelding and pictures attributed to Stubbs, Brooking, Poelenburgh, Weenix, Roos, Rubens and Vernet.

4 Original Correspondence of Ozias Humphry, MS. in library of the Royal Academy, vol. I, 134.

5 *Letters*, ed. Mrs. Paget Toynbee, vol. VIII (1904), p.207.

law, the queen may have listened on occasion to the enthusiastic descriptions of Florence by Lady Charlotte Finch, a close friend and governess to the royal children, who had spent many months in Florence as a girl, knew Zoffany well and was, indeed, inserted by him into the most delightful of all his royal conversation-pieces, the group formed by Queen Charlotte, seated on a bench in a park, surrounded by two of her brothers and three of her children.

This is not the occasion on which to present an anthology of the descriptions of the Medici collections by English visitors to Florence from the early seventeenth to the mid-eighteenth centuries, or to assess the inspiration it gave to English artists from the time of Nicholas Stone to the days of Ozias Humphry. Nor can one do more than glance at the fruitful tradition of painted cabinets and galleries of which Zoffany's picture was to become one of the most brilliant examples. The genre has a long and crowded history, predominantly in Flanders, going back to the sixteenth century;[1] and in almost all its manifestations there appears to have been a strong element of fantasy. When Jan Bruegel, for instance, painted fairly early in the history of the genre his pictures (in the Prado) of the pleasures of the Senses, an elaborate picture-gallery is obviously something in which our Sight [Plate 7]

1 The genre is fully discussed in S. Speth-Holterhoff, *Les Peintres Flamands de Cabinets d'Amateurs au XVII Siècle* (Brussels 1957).

Plate 7 Jan Bruegel *The Sense of Sight* Oil on canvas $68\frac{7}{8} \times 103\frac{1}{2}$ inches Prado Museum, Madrid

Plate 8 Giovanni Paolo Panini *The Classical Picture-Gallery* Oil on canvas $67\frac{1}{2} \times 91\frac{1}{2}$ inches
The Metropolitan Museum of Art, New York Gwynne M. Andrews Fund, 1952

Plate 9 David Teniers *The Gallery of the Archduke Leopold William* Oil on canvas
$37\frac{3}{4} \times 50\frac{3}{8}$ inches Bayerische Staatsgemäldesammlungen, Munich

Plate 10 Willem van Haecht *The Picture Gallery of Cornelis van der Geest* Oil on panel
39 × 53 inches Mrs Mary van Berg, New York

Plate 11 Gonzales Coques *The Picture Gallery of Jan van Baveghem* Oil on canvas
29¾ × 44¼ inches Reproduced by gracious permission of Her Majesty the Queen

1 The most striking essay by Panini in this genre is probably his view (1749) of the Gallery of Cardinal Valenti Gonzaga now in the Wadsworth Atheneum.

2 S. Speth-Holterhoff, op. cit., pp.181-3. The picture hung in Queen Charlotte's Work-room at Kew.

3 In the Panshanger MSS., now in the Hertfordshire County Record Office, kindly communicated to me by the County Archivist, Mr. Peter Walne.

4 The *Gazzetta Toscana*, the Florentine weekly, is full at this period of accounts of the lavish supper parties and elaborate musical entertainments given by Cowper.

5 Lady V. Manners and Dr. G. C. Williamson, *John Zoffany, R.A.*, (1920), p.54.

6 See Appendix B, I, II.

7 The best account of the Tribuna is D. Heikamp, 'Zur Geschichte der Uffizien-Tribuna...', *Zeitschrift für Kunstgeschichte*, Band 26, Heft 3/4 (Munich, Berlin, 1963), pp.193-268, and his 'La Tribuna degli Uffizi come era nel Cinquecento', *Antichità Viva*, no. 3 (Florence, 1964).

can take pleasure. Much later, in 1757, Panini creates [Plate 8] an airy classical temple in which to display classical remains and his own views of classical buildings and ruins.[1] Even in the most familiar pictures in this convention, Teniers's views of the gallery of the Archduke Leopold William in Brussels [e.g., Plate 9], the actual disposition of the paintings in the collection, and the form of the frames, are falsified in order to bring a great many famous pictures within the painter's scope. Perhaps the most important of all the pictures of galleries is William van Haecht's view (1628) of the picture-gallery of Cornelis van der Geest, painted to commemorate a visit by the Archduke Albert and the Archduchess Isabella [Plate 10]. It is very carefully composed and was clearly, so far as the portraits are concerned, composed from existing sources; it also illustrates the main *desiderata* in the grandest pictures of this kind: the owner and his distinguished visitors are grouped prominently in the design; nearby are other intelligent and appreciative visitors or friends – artists, savants and fellow-collectors; and specially prized or intriguing pictures are placed on the floor for reverend inspection. Queen Charlotte owned an interesting picture in this convention, the *Picture Gallery of Jan van Baveghem* by Gonzales Coques at Windsor [Plate 11]. It has been suggested[2] that the picture was painted for the owner of the collection, who was an advocate, by the artists whose cause he had championed. The pictures in it (some are signed and dated 1683) were actually inserted by the individual painters; the portraits are by Coques; and the elaborate decoration of the room was independently signed and dated by von Ehrenberg in 1674. This is, briefly, the convention in which Zoffany was to paint his picture for the queen.

On 23 June 1772 Lady Spencer wrote to Lord Cowper in Florence: 'I have the Queens Commands to recommend Zoffani a Painter & a very ingenious Man to your Lordships protection, Her Majesty sends him to Florence & wishes to have him admitted into the Great Dukes Gallery this I have no doubt will be a sufficient Motive for your Lordships gaining him every advantage in your power, but I cannot in justice to the Man help adding that he has uncommon Merit & has distinguish'd himself very much in his stile of Portrait Painting'.[3]

This is the moment at which to present the 3rd Earl Cowper, seen, in Zoffany's slightly later portrait [Plate 12], strolling through the grounds of the Villa Palmieri on the hillside below Fiesole. Since he had come to Italy in 1759 on the Grand Tour, he had settled in Florence; he was a friend of the Grand Duke and a leader in Florentine society.[4] He would use his influence with the Grand Duke on behalf of artists from England who wished to study or copy pictures in his collections. Not that there was any nonsense in his mind about the artist's place in society. It is related that Zoffany used to walk about Florence in a pink coat. To this Lord Cowper took exception as it made Zoffany look like an English Earl.[5]

The practical arrangements for Zoffany to work in the Uffizi Gallery were made, as they often were in such cases, by Sir Horace Mann, Envoy Extraordinary to the Tuscan Court. On 13 August 1772 he was officially informed that, in accordance with the Grand Duke's wishes, the Director of the Gallery had been asked to do all in his power to enable Zoffany to paint his view of the Tribuna in the Gallery.[6] It was, then, the Tribuna that Zoffany planned to paint, the room built in the Gallery in 1585-9 by Bernardo Buontalenti for Francesco de' Medici, but not completed until the reign of his successor, Ferdinando I: built, moreover, as the central shrine to contain many of the most celebrated, exotic and precious works of art in the Medici collections.[7] It had fascinated travellers ever since. In Zoffany's day much survived of the original decoration that has since been swept away. In his *Tribuna* [Plate 13], for example, Zoffany paints with meticulous accuracy the rich cornice of the room and the gold and mother-of-pearl arabesques on the blue lapis-lazuli of the cupola above; but the gay scarlet hangings, the skirting-board with the frieze, designed by Ligozzi, of birds, fish, shells, plants and stones, and the shelf with drawers, which ran

Plate 12 Johann Zoffany *George, 3rd Earl Cowper*
Oil on canvas 56 × 43¾ inches The Viscountess Gage

Plate 13 Johann Zoffany *The Tribuna of the Uffizi* Oil on canvas $48\frac{5}{8} \times 61$ inches
Reproduced by gracious permission of Her Majesty the Queen

round the room supported on carved and gilded consoles, all these original features in the room have long since disappeared. Zoffany's canvas provides, indeed, the best visual record of the Tribuna at a time when it still played its original part in the arrangements in the Gallery as a whole. It was still a realisation of Galileo's dream of 'una guardaroba, una tribuna, una galleria regia, ornata di cento statue antiche de' più celebri scoltori, con infinite storie intere, e le migliori, di pittori illustri, con un numero grande di vasi, di cristalli, d'agate, di lapis lazzari e d'altre gioie, e finalmente ripiene di cose rare, preziose, maravigliose e di tutta eccelenza'.[1] Smollett, seven years before Zoffany came to Florence, wrote of the Tribuna: 'There is such a profusion of curiosities in this celebrated musæum . . . that the imagination is bewildered . . . a stranger of a visionary turn would be apt to fancy himself in a palace of the fairies, raised and adorned by the power of inchantment'.[2]

In all its details Zoffany did not finish his picture until the end of 1777 or early in 1778. We shall see that he allowed himself to be diverted by other commissions. One press-

1 E. Panofsky, *Galileo as a Critic of the Arts* (The Hague, 1954), p.19. There is at Narford Hall a most interesting premonition of Zoffany's picture: a painting by Giulio Pignatta, signed and dated 1715, which shows Sir Andrew Fountaine and others in the Tribuna.

2 *Works*, ed. W. E. Henley, vol. XI (1900), p.298.

reporter stated, when the picture was finally exhibited at the Royal Academy in 1780, that 'it . . . employed Mr. Zoffani almost three years and an half '.[1] Zoffany himself stated that he had undertaken to finish it by Christmas 1772. This is barely credible; and one visitor to Florence was under the impression, in March 1773, that it could not be finished before June or July of that year. The visitor was the young Lord Winchilsea,[2] son of Zoffany's old acquaintance, Lady Charlotte Finch. His reactions to the Uffizi and the Tribuna are typical of a young man on the Grand Tour, fresh from Eton and Christ Church and, in his case, with no special feeling for the arts. At first we find him writing to his mother from Florence on 20 December 1772:

'. . . I really believe if I was to stay any time here I should have a kind of a taste for Statues & Paintings &c., but as yet I know so little about them, that I have not that pleasure other people have who understand them . . .'[3]

He writes later in a different strain:

'. . . I have been extremely well entertained here with seeing all the Multitude of things there are to be seen the Galery is the most delightfull thing possible I have passed all my mornings there & could if I was to stay a month longer, go there every morning without being the least tired of it. the Tribune which you must remember is quite a Paradise, for the first time of going there one is really quite confused & amazed with the profusion of things, & I am sure it would take a month to see compleatly that room only. Zoffani the Painter is here, I went to see his picture that he is doing, of the Tribune it is I think the Most Charming thing I ever saw, it is the Picture of the Room of the Tribune, & all the statues & Pictures are introduced in it . . . he is quite afraid he shall not be able to finish it so soon as he intended, as it is so very laborious a work, he desired me to mention that to you with a view I imagine of its being repeated [i.e, one presumes, to Queen Charlotte], it is really such a work as I have no Idea of any body's getting through in a year . . .'[4]

A fortnight later, on 2 January 1773, the Earl returns to the same theme:

'. . . I go every Morning into the Gallery which I admire more & more, I believe it is allowed to be one of the finest things in the World, the Tribune particularly is the most Charming thing I ever saw, it is that that Zoffani is drawing the Picture of which is really one of the Most laborious undertakings I ever saw. for he not only Copies a great Many Pictures & Statues & the Room &c. which is a great deal to do, but even the Frames & every the most minute thing Possible the small bronzes, the Table &c. to make it be a compleat & exact representation of the Room, & besides that he is obliged to put several of the Pictures in perspective, & to make a distinction between the life & the heads in the Pictures, & what is most difficult of all to make them appear as if they were painted on different Kinds of Canvass as in the Originals. When it is done it will be a very pretty thing, & will give a very good Idea of the Originals . . :'[5]

From Lord Winchilsea's enthusiastic comments it seems that by the end of 1772 Zoffany, within four months of starting work on the picture, had painted a considerable part – conceivably all – of the setting of the scene therein. If this was so, he must have worked with intense application during those first months in Florence. Indeed, when Zoffany was charged, after his return to London, with having stayed too long in Florence, he claimed that he 'had once been brought home with loss of power from intense study, that state of inanition being afterwards considered as the first seizure of paralysis, which some years later carried him to his grave'.[6] In Zoffany's words, too close an application was dangerous in that very cold stone building. It is not difficult to imagine the darkness and dankness in the Uffizi after the autumn rains had broken over the city. Zoffany may also have sought relief, in the overwork which brought on this sinister seizure, from his grief at the tragic death of his little son.[7]

1 *The London Courant*, 4 May 1780.

2 George Finch, 9th Earl of Winchilsea (1752–1826), Gentleman of the Bedchamber, 1777–1812, and Groom of the Stole, 1804–12.

3 Finch MSS., formerly at Burley-on-the-Hill, deposited in the Leicestershire County Record Office; no. 26 in the series of the 9th Earl of Winchilsea's letters to his mother. I am most grateful to Col. James Hanbury for giving me permission to quote from these letters.

4 Ibid., no. 27.

5 Ibid., no. 29.

6 *Court and Private Life in the Time of Queen Charlotte : being the Journals of Mrs. Papendiek*, ed. Mrs. V. Delves Broughton (1887), vol. I, p.84.

7 Ibid., vol. I, pp.87–88.

Plate 14 *The Tribuna* detail

†Such numbers refer to the keyed illustration at the end of the book.

1 See G. A. Mansuelli, *Galleria degli Uffizi, Le Sculture*, vol. I (Rome, 1958), nos. 45, 51, 55, 61.

2 Ibid., vol. I, no. 63.

3 Ibid., vol. I, no. 58; it can be seen in Benedetto de Greyss's view of this part of the Gallery (Plate 1).
   Permission was always readily given to artists who wished to sketch the statues in the Corridors (one sees a student drawing in De Greyss's view), but it was much more difficult to secure permission to draw or copy the statues in the Tribuna. Zoffany was accorded special privileges as he claimed to be Queen Charlotte's painter (Appendix B, III, IV).

4 Ozias Humphry's Original Correspondence, MS., in library of the Royal Academy, vol. II, 39, 41.

5 'Zoffany's painting of Charles Towneley's Library in Park Street', *Burlington Magazine*, vol. CVI (1964), pp.316–23.

Examination of the canvas reveals that Zoffany laid out the scene and furnished the stage before he brought on the players. The first task he set himself was to paint the walls and the shelves and to stand the six principal statues on the floor. The line of shelves is painted right round – or across – the canvas and is only broken at the four points where the statues stand in front of it and in the middle of the central wall where it was interrupted by the space occupied by a picture [see Plate 13]. At this stage in the work Zoffany was more or less strictly fulfilling the queen's commission 'to paint for Her, the Florence Gallery'. The six principal statues are the *Arrotino* or *Scita Scorticatore* [48],† *Cupid and Psyche* [49], the *Faun* or *Satyr* [50], *Hercules strangling the Serpent* [51], the *Wrestlers* [52] and the *Venus de' Medici* [53]. The *Venus*, the *Satyr*, the *Scita* and the *Wrestlers* had always been in the Tribuna;[1] the *Hercules*[2] was apparently in the Tribuna at that date and it too had been in the room when it was first arranged. But *Cupid and Psyche* was probably never in the Tribuna and in Zoffany's day was almost certainly in the *Seconda Galleria* of the Uffizi.[3] It is at once clear that Zoffany was already to a certain extent composing *his* Tribuna. To look ahead for a moment: Charles Towneley was in Florence in 1775–6 and was often in Zoffany's company;[4] Mrs Lightbown has recently shown that when Zoffany came to paint for him the famous picture of his library he once again created not an accurate portrait of a collection but 'a picturesque composition according to his own taste'.[5] X-ray [Plate 30] has only revealed one important change in the preliminary placing of the statues. The place now filled by the *Hercules* was at first occupied by a young male statue which Zoffany decided to paint out, perhaps because it would have interfered with our view of the

Plate 15 a, b, c *The Tribuna* three details

painting behind it. This statue was almost certainly the *Apollino*[1] which had always stood in the Tribuna and still stands there on one of the fine carved and gilded bases that Zoffany paints so carefully under three of his statues.

On the shelves running round the walls Zoffany places a collection of smaller classical and renaissance works of art. The effect is rather the same in general as the collection that was actually there [see Plate 15abc], but he seems to have varied it considerably in detail. He also understandably brought on to these shelves works of art which were standing on the shelves that were out of his vision. I have only succeeded in identifying in Florence a small number of the objects Zoffany arranged on the shelves and I am sure that further search in the Museo degli Argenti would bring more of them to light. The first bust on the left is the so-called *Plautilla* [69]; on the right of the *Satyr* can be seen the bust of *Annius Verus* [72];[2] and the smaller works between them include two small precious heads [70, 71] now in the Museo degli Argenti, of which one is the *Tiberius* in blue jaspar, set on a gold bust made in Florence in the sixteenth century. Balancing the *Annius Verus*, and on the right of the central space, is the bust once described as the young *Nero* [73];[3] moving along to the right of the picture the identifiable pieces are a small bronze *Hercules* [74], in the Museo Archeologico, a little egg-shaped, Egyptian-headed figure [75] in the Museo degli Argenti and Bertoldo's *Arion* [76], which is now in the Bargello. Zoffany occasionally shifted these small objects on the shelves as the composition developed and some were clearly painted after the picture-frames behind them had been finished.

1 Mansuelli, op. cit., vol. I, no. 46.

2 Both are in the Uffizi: Mansuelli, op. cit., vol. II, nos. 141, 104.

3 Ibid., vol. II, no. 60.

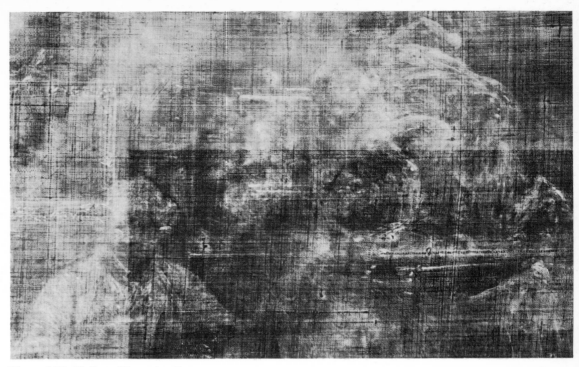

Plate 16 *The Tribuna* X-ray detail

1 The series of drawings was begun in 1748 in the time of the Grand Duke Francesco Stefano under the direction of Benedetto de Greyss, took many years and was never completed; Gibbon saw some of them being made in 1764. The drawings of the walls of the Tribuna are in the Gabinetto dei Disegni in the Uffizi nos. 4579-4588 bis.).

2 Dr. Doran, '*Mann' and Manners at the Court of Florence* (1876), vol. II, pp.358-60. Mr. Warren H. Smith most kindly provided me with corrections to Dr. Doran's text of the letter.

3 The inventory is preserved in the archives of the Gallery. The pictures in the Tribuna are nos. 1074-1188; nos. 1189-1418 are the statues and small objects 'che si ritrovano sui seguenti Palchetti'. The following are the nos. of the pictures identifiable in Zoffany's picture, with nos. from the key in square brackets: 1093[47], 1117[36] as a Holbein of Luther, 1118[35], 1142[29] as by Titian, 1149[38], 1151[31], 1156[41], 1169[42] as by Caravaggio, 1175[32], 1176[30], 1179[34] as by Raphael, 1181[27], 1183[23], 1188[26].

4 See Appendix B, V.

In painting the pictures, however, X-ray [Plate 16] has shown only one alteration during the growth of the picture: the place now filled by the *Holy Family* [37], which seems in Zoffany's time not to have been in the Tribuna and to have been attributed to Perugino, was at first taken by a much smaller, and now unidentifiable, picture. In order to see how Zoffany arranged – or rearranged – the pictures hanging on the walls, it is convenient to compare his picture with the three relevant drawings from the series of carefully drawn records of the walls in the Grand Duke's Gallery.[1] I have joined three of these drawings together on one Plate [17] so that the comparison can be made more easily. The three walls that Zoffany tackled were those on the north-east side of the room, on the left of the room, that is, if you enter the Tribuna through the original door from the Corridor; in Zoffany's day that was still the only entrance to the room.

In Sir Horace Mann's long and very important letter to Walpole of 10 December 1779,[2] after Walpole had had an opportunity to see the picture, he wrote that, as 'Her Majesty's Painter', Zoffany 'had leave to have any Picture in the Gallery or Palace taken down; for you must have observed that he has transported some from the latter place [i.e., the Pitti] into his Tribune'. Twenty pictures are clearly visible in Zoffany's Tribuna. Of these, fourteen were in the Tribuna in the inventory of the Uffizi in 1769.[3] In the archives of the Uffizi is the list of pictures that Zoffany included in his picture.[4] In it are seven pictures stated to have come from the Pitti: the *Cleopatra* [38] and the *Charity* [24] by Guido, Allori's *Miracle of St Julian* [43], two pictures by Rubens, the *Self-portrait with Lipsius and his pupils* [39] and the *Horrors of War* [33], and Raphael's *Leo X* [40] and *Madonna della Sedia* [25]. These are worked into the places of the pictures which Zoffany had chosen to discard from his Tribuna.

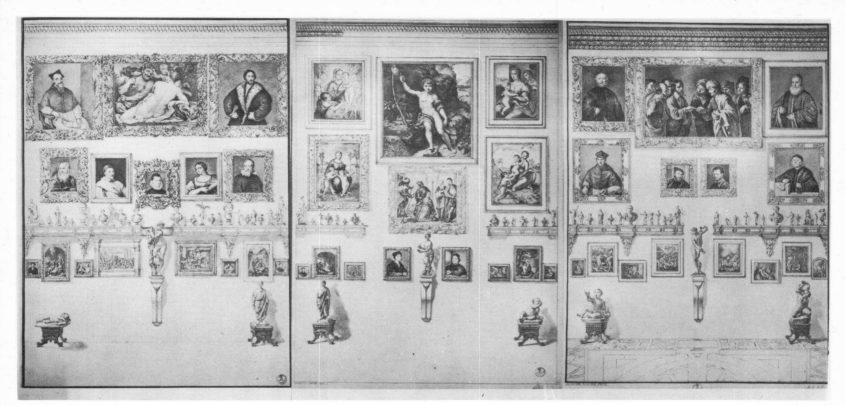

Plate 17 Giuseppe Magni *Three drawings of the north-east walls of the Tribuna*
Gabinetto dei Disegni, Uffizi, Florence

A glance at the official drawings [Plates 17–19], which show the walls as they were not long before Zoffany arrived in Florence, shows that Zoffany kept at least one picture from each wall. On the left wall he retained Carracci's *Baccante* [23] and the Sustermans of Galileo [27]. On the central wall he placed, on either side of Raphael's *St John* [30], the two *Madonnas* [32 and 34; the latter is now regarded as by Franciabigio]; and below them he kept Holbein's *Sir Richard Southwell* [35] and its companion [36], now described as a portrait by Raphael of Perugino, then as a portrait of Luther by Holbein. He may have moved over on to his left wall [28] the old copy, still in the Uffizi, of Rembrandt's *Holy Family* in the Louvre; this is seen in the drawing below the *Madonna del Cardellino*. Zoffany brings into his vision one picture [29] from a wall on the other side of the room [Plate 18]; a turn of ninety degrees would have brought Zoffany face to face with a niche in the wall occupied by a famous cabinet and by Michelangelo's Tondo [Plate 19]. This would have been a difficult wall to paint unless Zoffany had made it the centre of his design; but as a pupil of Mengs Zoffany would naturally have given the place of honour, not to Michelangelo, but to Raphael.

Into the framework of pictures that he wished to retain in his Tribuna Zoffany fitted the masterpieces from the Pitti. There was inevitably some distortion in the relative scale of the paintings he presented. On the left wall there is practically no such distortion. On the right wall the relative sizes of the top row are almost exactly correct (Pietro da Cortona's *Abraham and Hagar* [41] is a bit too large in relation to Guido's *Cleopatra* [38] above); but the whole scale was distorted by Zoffany's decision to bring on to this wall the huge Allori [43] from the Pitti, which is in fact 107 cm. higher and 78 cm. wider than the Raphael [40] above it. The central wall involved the biggest distortion of all. The five framed pictures are cor-

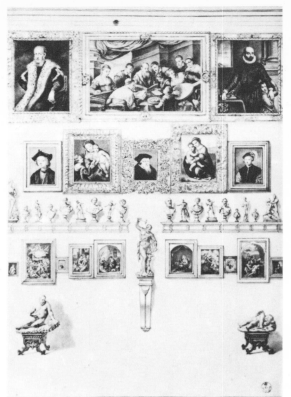

Plate 18 Giuseppe Magni *Drawing of a wall of the Tribuna* Gabinetto dei Disegni, Uffizi, Florence

Plate 19 Giuseppe Magni *Drawing of a wall of the Tribuna* Gabinetto dei Disegni, Uffizi, Florence

rectly shown in scale, but the scale was completely thrown out when Zoffany replaced Veronese's *Martyrdom of St Justina*, which neatly fits the space below Raphael's *St John*, with the big Rubens [33] from the Pitti. The Rubens is actually 195 cm. wider than the Raphael and it would be impossible for it to be fitted, flanked by the two smaller pictures [32 and 34], on one of the walls of the Tribuna.

The most obvious effect of Zoffany's 'improvements' in the Tribuna is to make the selection of pictures gayer and livelier. There are now only three small single portraits to be seen where the official drawings apparently have seventeen. His choice of pictures also makes the collection a little more modern, bringing in Pietro da Cortona and Rubens and increasing the showing of Guido Reni. Venetian painting, on the other hand, is played right down, but an anthology of paintings that brings in Pietro da Cortona and two large canvases by Rubens was clearly not based on rigidly classical tastes. Pietro da Cortona's *Abraham and Hagar* [41] may have been brought in to illustrate the admiration still felt in Florence for his superb decorations in the Pitti. The principal result of Zoffany's changes is, however, an even louder paean of praise in honour of Raphael than we could catch from the drawings. Perhaps we should give some credit for this to Giuseppe Pelli Bencivenni who in 1773 succeeded Giuseppe Querci as Director or *Primo Custode* of the Gallery. He must have had many conversations with Zoffany and watched him, and helped him, at his work. In 1779 he published in Florence in two volumes his fascinating *Saggio Istorico* of the Grand Duke's collection. He made use of the archives of the Uffizi. He would perhaps have told Zoffany that the inventory of the Tribuna in 1589 included Raphael's *Madonna della Sedia* [25], *Leo X with the Cardinals* [40] and *St John* [30]. This may have encouraged Zoffany to bring back the first two of them from the Pitti. Bencivenni describes the Grand Duke's unrivalled collection of Raphaels: 'è il sovrano più ricco di quadri di *Raffaello*'. Taking the *Madonna del Cardellino* [32], the other *Madonna* [34] and *St John* [30] as examples of three phases in Raphael's development, he writes: 'Lo studio di questi tre quadri è la scuola più grande che possa avere un pittore, e se sarebbe preziosi distintamente presi, aumentano di merito a stare assieme in confronto, perchè indicano le vestigia che calcò il più gran genio che nascesse dopo il risorgimento dell'arte'. This is the dream which Zoffany realises for us.[1]

Now 'small figures (portraits) as Spectators'[2] had been conceived as part of the original idea for the picture, but at an early stage in its development Zoffany must have decided to assemble in his Tribuna a conversazione of a very unusual and imaginative kind. In the letter in which Lord Winchilsea described to his mother what Zoffany was doing in his picture, he told her that beside the statues and pictures 'are the Pictures of several young men that have been here, as Ld Plymouth M^r F: Harvey, Ld Cooper, Mr Dashwood 2 Mr Wilbraham S^r H Mann & two men that shew the Pictures'. He goes on, underlining his words as his excitement rises: 'he asked me *to be in it* which *I am* accordingly to be & have set once already & it is very like my other Picture . . .'[3] At this time, late in 1772 or early in 1773, Zoffany was painting, therefore, the little group of figures round the *Venus de' Medici* [Plate 20]: Lord Winchilsea [13], the two Mr Wilbrahams [14 and 21], Mr Watts [15] and Mr Doughty [16]. Mr Doughty may have been added very slightly later to the others.[4] On the other side of the room Zoffany had placed Lord Cowper [1], Lord Plymouth [3][5] and Valentine Knightley [10] gazing at the *Satyr* [Plate 21]. By 14 February 1773 he had also introduced Charles Loraine-Smith [5] sketching *Cupid and Psyche*.[6] Lord Winchilsea,

Plate 20 *The Tribuna* detail

1 G. P. Bencivenni, *Saggio Istorico della Real Galleria di Firenze* (Florence, 1779), vol. I, pp.187, 190–1.

2 Letter from Mann to Walpole, 25 August 1772, reporting Zoffany's arrival in Florence, 'sent by a great Personage' to paint 'a perspective view of the Tribuna' (Doran, op. cit., vol. II, p.236).

3 Finch MSS., no. 27 of Lord Winchilsea's letters

4 Ibid., no. 29. Winchilsea to his mother, 2 January 1773: '. . . we have hardly any English here at present Mr Knightley the Youngest Brother, Mr Watts, Mr May, & 2 Mr Wilbrahams'.
　Mr. Knightley [10] was probably Valentine Knightley (1744–96) of Fawsley, who is presumably the Knightley who was in Florence in November 1772; a man of this name left Florence in March or April 1773 and took back with him from Mann to Walpole a bundle of Walpole's letters. The two Wilbrahams were probably two of the sons of Roger Wilbraham of Nantwich: Thomas (b. 1751), George (1741–1813) or Roger (1743–1829). A portrait of Roger Wilbraham bears a resemblance to no. 14; he was F.S.A. and F.R.S. and owned a fine library of Italian and Spanish books, partly collected on his travels. No. 14 also resembles a figure called 'Mr. Wilbraham' in a caricature group by Patch at Floors Castle. I have not so far satisfactorily identified Watts or Doughty.

5 Other Windsor, 6th Earl of Plymouth (1751–99). He was in Florence in 1772, but had probably left by the end of the year, as he was painted in that year in Rome by Pompeo Batoni. Mann described him as 'the most sweet temper and fat body I ever knew. What a sad prospect at his age of being immovable before he is thirty'. The temper and body are alike evident in Batoni's portrait.

6 Finch MSS., no. 32 of Lord Winchilsea's letters, written on 16 February 1773: '. . . Smith & Doughty left this ye day before yesterday morning much against Smith's inclination but Doughty was so tired ye he would not stay any longer, upon any terms . . . there are now but 4 English, 2 Mr Wilbrahams Mr Knightley & myself . . .'. In his previous letter, no. 31, of 1 February 1773, Lord Winchilsea had written: '. . . Mr Doughty the other day received three letters the first he had had from the time he left England. & it is now 3 months since Mr Smith has had any . . .'
　Charles Loraine-Smith (1751–1835), second son of Sir Charles Loraine, 3rd Bt., is the only example of the amateur artist in Zoffany's picture. He was also a famous fox-hunting country gentleman and gave Morland asylum on his estate at Enderby in Leicestershire. 'A nice, critical observer of elegant structures and classic scenery', he 'directed Morland in the choice of such remarkable figures, striking views, and sequestered situations, as would appear best suited to the vivacity of design and freedom, of a light, ready hand' (J. Hassell, *Memoirs of the Life of the late George Morland* (1806), pp.17–18). When

Loraine-Smith ceased looking at the coverts of the Quorn through the eyes of Gaspar Poussin, he descended – if it was a descent – to the vernacular tradition of the sporting print. In this genre his masterpiece is the print laconically entitled *The Loss of the Chaplain* (*The Field*, Christmas number, 1920; W. Shaw Sparrow, *British Sporting Artists from Barlow to Herring* (1922), pp.150–1).

Plate 21 *The Tribuna* detail

1 Ibid. When Lord Winchilsea eventually arrived in Rome he did not sit to Pompeio: the painter was very busy and an attack of ague had lent a yellowish tinge to the Earl's complexion which he did not wish to be transmitted to posterity (no. 36 of his letters, from Rome, 17 April 1773).

2 *The Autobiographies of Edward Gibbon*, ed. J. Murray (1896), p.267.

3 *Gibbon's Journey from Geneva to Rome*, ed. G. A. Bonnard (1961), p.179.
   The identity of the young man [9] standing behind Valentine Knightley [10] is not established. The early Key identifies him as Lord Russborough, i.e., Joseph Leeson, Viscount Russborough and 2nd Earl of Milltown (1730–1801). But the sitter is surely too young for Lord Russborough and bears no resemblance to the portrait of him by Batoni (1751) in the National Gallery of Ireland.

4 Finch MSS, no. 33 of Lord Winchilsea's letters. From Rome he wrote to his mother on 26 April 1773, asking her to tell his sister Sophia 'that my second face in Zoffani's Picture is certainly not so like as the first by a great deal, I don't go by my own Judgement but by everybody else's...'

who had promised his mother that he would sit to Batoni when he arrived in Rome, was sure that the Roman painter could not equal Zoffany's ability to catch a likeness: '... I will certainly give Pompeio a very good setting at Rome & wish he may succeed. but you will see a much liker one I dare say in Zoffani's picture in which I am they tell me the likest Picture that was ever done Mʳ Smith & Mʳ Doughty are there also and very like particularly Mʳ Doughty. Mʳ Knightley's too is exactly him...'[1]

The original conception of his picture in Zoffany's mind thus seems to have included two small groups of visitors to the Gallery absorbed in contemplation of the *Satyr, Cupid and Psyche* and the *Venus de' Medici*. Lord Winchilsea and his young companions would have agreed with Gibbon. 'In the Gallery, and especially in the Tribune, I first acknowledged, at the feet of the Venus of Medicis, that the chisel may dispute the pre-eminence with the pencil, a truth in the fine arts which cannot on this side of the Alps be felt or understood':[2] an epitome of an experience which he had described in warmer tones in his Journal: 'quand on voit la VENUS DE MEDICIS, on fait peu d'attention à la chambre qui la contient.... C'est la sensation la plus voluptueuse que mon oeil ait jamais eprouvé'.[3] A modification, however, became necessary. On 9 March 1773 Lord Winchilsea wrote to his mother in a despondent tone:

'... Zoffani's Picture won't be finished a good while yet I should think it would take him three or four Months more,... he had done my picture very like but was obliged to rub it out as he had made it too high I have set once for the second but don't think it will be as like as yᵉ first...'[4]

X-ray [Plate 22] clearly shows the first edition of Lord Winchilsea's head a few inches above the second, and final, version of it. It also shows, between this first head and the thighs of Venus, another head – and, indeed, much of the torso – of another spectator who is now concealed behind, and slightly above, Mr Doughty [16]. The impasto on his white cravat can be seen going across Mr Doughty's brow. In the long letter he wrote to Walpole on 10 December 1779, Mann said that:

'I told him often of the impropriety of sticking so many figures in it, and pointed out to him, the Great Duke and Dutchess, one or two of their children, if he thought the variety

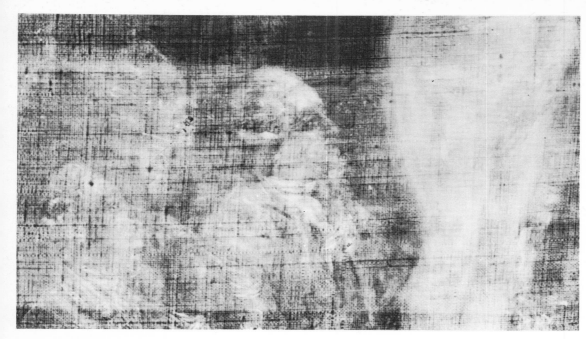

Plate 22 *The Tribuna* X-ray detail

more pictoresk, and Lord Cowper. He told me that the King had expressly ordered mine to be there, which I did not believe, but did not object to it; but he made the same merit with all the young travellers then at Florence, some of whom he afterwards rubbed out, as old Felton Harvey and one of the Queen's Chaplains with a broad black ribbon across his forehead, and filled up their places elsewhere. If what he said is true, that the Queen sent him to Florence to do that picture, and gave him a large sum for his journey, the impropriety of crowding in so many unknown figures was still greater'.

The painted-out figure does not appear to be the Queen's Chaplain. Was it, perhaps, the Mr Dashwood whom Lord Winchilsea had noted in the picture? It is possible that Mann made a mistake in telling Walpole that Felton Hervey[1] had been painted out. The early key to the picture, produced when it was shown at the British Institution in 1814, states that the elderly figure [17] seated in black in the foreground was Felton Hervey; the figure bears a reasonable resemblance to the portrait of him by Fayram at Ickworth, though this was admittedly painted much earlier; and it tallies with contemporary descriptions of him as 'very pale and Roman nosed' and 'vastly awkward and ungainly'.

The group in the foreground [Plate 23] probably consisted at first of Felton Hervey [17], Thomas Patch [18][2] and Sir Horace Mann [20].[3] It is possible that Patch was mistaken by Lord Winchilsea for one of the 'two men that shew the Pictures'. There is even a curious confusion over the figure of Mann. He is definitely stated by Lord Winchilsea, in his letter of 27 December 1772, to be already in the picture; Felton Hervey's glance is unintelligible without the figure of Mann; but not until 28 September 1773 did Sir Horace himself write to Walpole: 'Mr Zoffany is now waiting for me in the next room, to put my portrait into the Picture which the King sent him hither to make of the *Tribuna* of the Gallery. It is a most curious and laborious undertaking'.[4] It is possible that Zoffany had laid in the figure which was to be placed there but did not get a sitting from Mann till much later.

Almost in the centre of the room, in front of the famous table (now in the Opeficio delle Pietre Dure in Florence) which was designed by Pocetti and Jacopo Ligozzi and was completed in 1649, stands a *Custode* [11] who holds up for the inspection of the group in the foreground one of the most ravishing jewels in the Grand Duke's inheritance, Titian's

1 Felton Hervey (1712-73), ninth son of the 1st Earl of Bristol. Equerry to Queen Caroline of Ansbach and Groom of the Bedchamber to William, Duke of Cumberland. He was in Florence early in September 1772. His pictures were sold at Christie's 3 and 4 February 1775.

2 Painter (1725-82) of caricatures and topographical views.

3 Mann (1706–88) was, as early as 1738, assisting the British Resident at the Grand Duke's court; in 1740 he succeeded to the post. In 1765 he was created Envoy Extraordinary and in 1782 he became Envoy Extraordinary and Plenipotentiary. In Zoffany's picture he wears the ribbon and star of the Bath which he had received in 1768.

4 Dr. Doran, op. cit., vol. II, p.245.

Plate 23 *The Tribuna* detail

Venus of Urbino [47]. In the official list of pictures included by Zoffany in his design[1] it is stated that among the portraits was 'il can. Querci'. This was Giuseppe Querci who in 1769 had succeeded Giuseppe Bianchi as *Custode* of the Gallery. Querci died in 1773 and the list states that after his death he was 'Levato', from the design. He may originally have been somewhere else in the design – it is conceivable that he is the figure painted out below Mr Doughty – but it is possible that he was shown holding the Titian and that after his death the Titian was placed 'fra Le mani del Bastianelli'.[2]

1 Appendix B, V.

2 Pietro Bastianelli was perhaps one of the senior *custodi* of the Gallery; in July 1792 he was still on the strength as a *custode*. The early Key to the picture states that the man holding the Titian is Giuseppe Bianchi, who had been dismissed in 1769. The whole of the *Venus of Urbino* was put on to the canvas and Felton Hervey's right arm was painted over part of it.

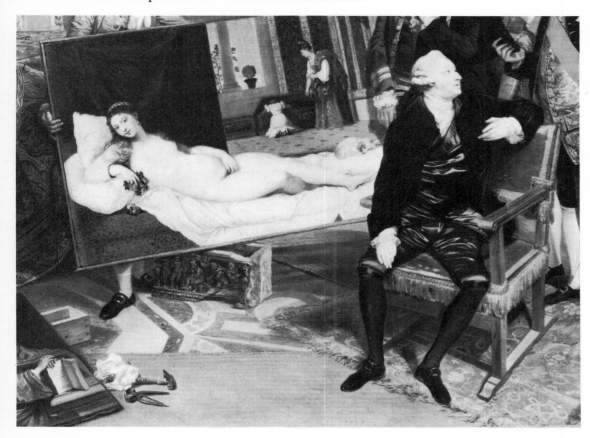

Plate 24 *The Tribuna* detail

The prominent display of Titian's ravishing *Venus* as the *chef-d'œuvre* of the collection, out of its frame [Plate 24], is in keeping with the demands of the genre to which Zoffany's picture belongs. It also demonstrates the special privileges granted to Zoffany as Queen Charlotte's painter. The Grand Duke Pietro Leopoldo was devoted to his collection and made important additions to it. He was generous in allowing students and artists to work and copy among his possessions.[3] But the Venus was, perhaps, one of the two most celebrated pieces in his collection; and by August 1772, although scaffolds or ladders could be provided for the serious student or copyist, she could not be taken off the walls.[4] Romney was disappointed in Florence in 1775:

'. . . On my arrival in Florence I met with letters to Lord Cowper and Sir Horace Mann: they seemed very desirous to serve me, but it was out of their power; the Grand Duke will not suffer the Venus to be taken down, nor any picture in the Pitti palace; alleging, that if he suffer any one he cannot refuse others, which he had done lately to two or three who had applied through very great interest. In order to recompence myself, I got a ladder and examined them very near several times, and found more information than I expected. I was very much entertained, and I believe employed my time to greater advantage, in making

3 Bencivenni wrote of him: 'Sapeva . . . che le magnifiche, e preziose collezioni di cose rare non devono essere una mostra di opulenza, ma un utile deposito che conservi, e propaghi la cultura dello spirito, combatta la sempre infelice, e dannosa ignoranza, e richiami la folla dei viaggiatori, i quali la lusinga di pascere l'anima con la vista delle cose belle, invita a passare, e trattenersi presso quei populi che le possiedono, per dividerne con essi il godimento'. (*Saggio Istorico*, op. cit., vol. I, pp.406–7).

4 Appendix B, VI.

1 Rev. J. Romney, *Memoirs of the Life and Works of George Romney* (1830), p.118.

2 Letter from Lord Cowper to Humphry, 20 May 1775 (Original Correspondence, op. cit., vol. II, 30). A letter from Humphry (Ibid., vol. I, 134), describing his journey to Rome in the early summer of 1773, includes a reference to Zoffany and his picture, to the miniature-like copies in it and to the 'great number of portraits of most the English gentlemen who have occasionally passed thro Florence'.

3 On 2 July 1774 the *Gazzetta Toscana* reported that a *sig. Gordon* was in Florence; he was perhaps identical with *Monsieur Gordon Uffiziale Inghilese*, reported in Florence on 13 August 1774. Sir John Taylor (d. 1786), created a Baronet in 1778, was in Rome in 1773 and is probably to be identified with a Taylor who was in Florence in November 1772.

4 On 11 January 1774 Bruce wrote to Sir Joseph Banks from Florence that Zoffany 'whom I have the pleasure to have met here' was forwarding on his behalf a letter to Lord North praying that his African drawings should be allowed to pass through the Customs free of duty. Four days later Zoffany wrote on behalf of Bruce (*The Banks Letters*, ed. W. R. Dawson (1958), p.177; W. T. Whitley, *Artists and their Friends in England 1700-1799*, vol. I, pp.295-6).

5 MS. Commonplace Book, communicated to me by Captain Marendaz in 1949.

6 Dr. Doran, op. cit., vol. II, p.274.

7 Whitley, op. cit., vol. I, pp.313-14, vol. II, p.310.

8 MS. sold at Sotheby's, 25 January 1955 (410), now in the Institut Néerlandais in Paris.

sketches from the works of Cimabue, Masaccio, Andrea del Sarto, and Michael Angelo . . .'[1]

Ozias Humphry, on the other hand, succeeded, through Lord Cowper's mediation with the Grand Duke, in getting permission to copy the *Venus* and the *Madonna della Sedia*.[2]

Into the group in the foreground Zoffany introduced, probably at different times, a Mr Gordon [12] and Sir John Taylor [19].[3] By the end of 1773 much of his Tribuna must have been completed; indeed, he was hoping to be able to finish it in March 1774. He continued to develop it and we have glimpses of him at work. In January 1774 James Bruce [22], the famous explorer, was in Florence[4] and Zoffany introduced 'this great man; the wonder of his age, the terror of married men, and a constant lover', into the group round the *Venus de' Medici*. In the same month Lord Clive was in Florence. He, wrote Zoffany heartlessly, 'should have liked a picture similar to that I am now painting of the Tribuna, but poor man, he could not go to the expense'. On 3 April 1774 the architect Edward Stevens wrote to Nollekens from Florence, where he had seen Zoffany at work on the picture.[5] On 23 August 1774 Mann wrote to Walpole: 'The one-eyed German, Zoffany, has succeeded amazingly well in many parts of [the picture], and in many portraits he has made here. The former is too much crouded with (for the most part) uninteresting Portraits of English travellers then here'.[6] When Reynolds's *Self-portrait* was placed in the Grand Duke's Gallery in 1775, 'Zoffany, among others, could not refrain from running to embrace it', although by 1778 he was talking maliciously of its present defects and future disintegration.[7] On 22 January 1775 Romney wrote from Florence to Ozias Humphry; he had dined with Zoffany and his family and Zoffany 'talks still of visiting Rome before he leaves Italy'.[8]

The 'many portraits he has made here' indicate that Zoffany now felt himself free to take on other commissions, but by staying on in Florence he was running the risk of his royal

Plate 25 Johann Zoffany *George, 3rd Earl Cowper, with the family of Charles Gore*
Oil on canvas 29½ × 37 inches The Hon. Lady Salmond

patrons' anger when he should decide to return to London. He had painted companion single portraits of Lord Cowper [Plate 12] and his Countess.[1] Just before their marriage on 2 June 1775 he painted her [Plate 25] with her parents and sisters; Lord Cowper gazes up at her from behind her father's chair; she stands in front of a picture of an auspicious Hymeneal scene; and in the background is a view of the hills round Florence. Maria Hadfield reported to Ozias Humphry, in a letter written from Florence on 24 February 1776, that Zoffany had begun a portrait (presumably the one now in Vienna) of the Empress Maria Theresa's daughter Maria Christina and had almost finished a portrait of Count Orlov.[2] The Empress had also commissioned Zoffany to paint a large conversation-piece or group-portrait [Plate 26] of the Grand Duke with his wife and children. In the late summer of 1776 he took this picture himself to Vienna, where the finishing touches had to be applied to it;[3] in design, and of course in Zoffany's use of seventeenth-century costumes, the group is closely akin to his Van Dyckian groups of the English royal family.[4]

By 15 April 1777 Zoffany was back in Florence and once more at work in the Gallery. A young Swiss nobleman, Louis-François, Baron Guiguer de Prangins, was travelling in Italy with his aunt and his two English cousins, Selina and Matilda Cleveland. Immediately after they had arrived in Florence they went 'chercher dans la Gallerie un peintre de portraits connu de nos Anglaises, Mr. Zoffani; il est bientôt décidé que ce sera lui que ma cousine Sélina emploiera pour faire le portrait en pied de ma cousine Matilda'. Sittings were given to Zoffany on 16, 17, 18, 22, 23, 28 April and also on 3 May. On 17 April the Baron wrote:

1 The portrait of Lady Cowper also belongs to Lady Gage.

2 Original Correspondence, op. cit., vol. II, 42. Zoffany was painting the Archduchess Maria Christina for the Empress in Florence in February 1776 (Briefe der Kaiserin Maria Theresia an ihre Kinder und Freunde, ed. A. R. von Arneth (Vienna, 1881), vol. II, p.402).

3 'Essendosi degnata S. M. l'Imperatrice Regina Apostolica d'incaricare il celebre Pittore Inglese Sig. Sophani, che da più anni addietro si trattiene in questa Capitale per copiare di commissione del Rè della Gran Brettagna suo Sovrano le opere di più eccellenti penelli che esistono in questa Real Galleria, di lavorare un Quadro in cui si contengano i ritratti de Reali nostri Sovrani, ed Arciduchi, e Arciduchesse, loro figli; fino di venerdì fera partì egli alla volta dell' Imperial Regia Corte di Vienna portando seco in un commodo carro fatto espressamente costruire il quadro suddetto, che egli colà dee terminare per quel che riguarda il volto di S.A.R. il Serenissimo Granduca. Tutte le persone dell'Arte che hanno veduta questa pittura unanimemente affermano, che, e per l'invenzione, e per l'esecuzione, è degna di stare al paragone delle più rinomate opere del secolo decimosetto' (Gazzetta Toscana, 31 August 1776).
   Bencivenni was equally enthusiastic. 'Io penso ancora di poter dare in questa mia Istoria la notizia di un quadro colorito per ordine della regina d'Inghilterra da Gio. Zoffany [note: Egli ha nel 1778. riposto alla Galleria il suo ritratto lavorato con spirito, e bravura] egregio pittore nato in Aquisgrana, e dall' imperatrice regina Maria Teresa creato cavaliere del sacro Romano impero in ricompensa della superba tela, nella quale ritrasse tutta la real famiglia di Toscana al naturale. E' il detto quadro un'opera in cui spicca con maraviglia il genio, la capacità, e la diligenza del professore che ha saputo in uno spazio poco maggiore di due braccia in altezza, e di un braccio e mezzo in larghezza ricopiare in prospettiva la stanza detta la Tribuna con le più eccellenti pitture che possiede il G.D. tanto nella Galleria, che nel real palazzo [note: Sono queste pitture in num. di 23, e ne ho io serbata la memoria nella filza V. di negozi ac. 26 dell archivio della Galleria] e con varie statue più celebri, situandovi di più in figura di spettatori molti personaggi espressi al vivo, con quella maestria, e verità che per altre opere è conosciuta in questo artefice' (Saggio Istorico, op. cit., vol. I, pp.441-2).

4 Farington records (Diary, ed. J. Greig, vol. I, (1923), p.204) that the Emperor Joseph II met Zoffany while he was at work on the picture. 'The next morning the grand Duke sent for Zoffany and engaged him to paint whole lengths of the Imperial family large as the life – ordered a table to be kept for him, & dresses to be made up to his taste for each figure to be painted'.

Plate 26 Johann Zoffany *Pietro Leopoldo, Grand Duke of Tuscany, with his Family*
Oil on canvas $127\frac{7}{8} \times 156\frac{5}{8}$ inches Kunsthistoriches Museum, Vienna

1 These extracts from the Baron's MS. 'Journal de Voyage en Italie' were most kindly sent to me by Professor Georges A. Bonnard.

'Le portrait sera charmant, et cette forme est mille fois plus agréable que la miniature sur une boite, ou la tête seule de grandeur naturelle. La figure sera entière, environ 15 pouces d' hauteur, assise sous des arbres, et une vue de Toscane dans l'éloignement'.[1]

From his description of it one can perhaps identify as the lost portrait of Matilda Cleveland the charming small full-length, hitherto described as of an unknown lady [Plate 27], in the Hyde collection in New York.

Plate 27 Johann Zoffany *Matilda Cleveland* Oil on canvas $22\frac{1}{2} \times 17\frac{1}{4}$ inches The late Mr Donald Hyde

At the end of 1777 Lord Lewisham [8] and his companion, Mr Stevenson [7], were in Florence.[1] Zoffany put them into his picture, where they join Charles Loraine-Smith who for five years has been making his sketch of *Cupid and Psyche*. Over his shoulder now peers a thirteen-year-old boy, Richard Edgcumbe [6]:[2] perhaps the most charming piece of genre painting in the whole design [Plate 28]. This newly-arrived trio – Lord Lewisham, Mr Stevenson and Richard Edgcumbe – are apparently unaware of the strange episode

1 George Legge, Lord Lewisham, later 3rd Earl of Dartmouth (1755-1810), Lord of the Bedchamber to the Prince of Wales, 1782-3, Lord Chamberlain, 1804-10. He had embarked on a continental tour with Mr. Stevenson in July 1775. Sir William Hamilton wrote, 'I cannot find the least fault in him, except his outside is a little too fat'. Sir William thought Stevenson 'as proper a companion for a young man as any I have ever seen in that situation'. The evidence of their being in Florence by 2 December 1777 is to be found in his letter to the Hon. T. Pelham, British Museum, Add. MSS. 33127, f.359, a reference most kindly given to me by Mr. Brinsley Ford.

2 Richard, later 2nd Earl of Mount Edgcumbe (1764-1839). A man of musical and artistic tastes. His serious travels on the Continent began in 1784 and I have found no evidence of his presence in Florence at an earlier date.

Plate 28 *The Tribuna* detail

behind them: unaware, that is, of Zoffany offering up Raphael's '*Niccolini*' *Madonna* [45] for inspection [Plate 21 and Frontispiece]. It is clear that Zoffany had been buying and selling pictures while he was in Florence. On 29 February 1775 Romney wrote from Venice to Charles Greville about his attempts to buy pictures for Lord Warwick: 'At Florence Mr. Zoffani has the first intelligence if there be any thing of value to be sold; sometime ago he made a purchase of four or five very good pictures, which are now in Lord Cowper's collection'.[3] Among them was the '*Niccolini*' *Madonna*, which remained with Lord Cowper's descendants at Panshanger until it was bought for the National Gallery in Washington. In order to fit in this transaction (we do not, unfortunately, know the exact dates on which Zoffany acquired the *Madonna* and sold it to the Earl) Zoffany had to make some alterations to his design. Lord Cowper [1] now points with his left arm to his new acquisition, although

3 Rev. J. Romney, op. cit., pp.113-14.

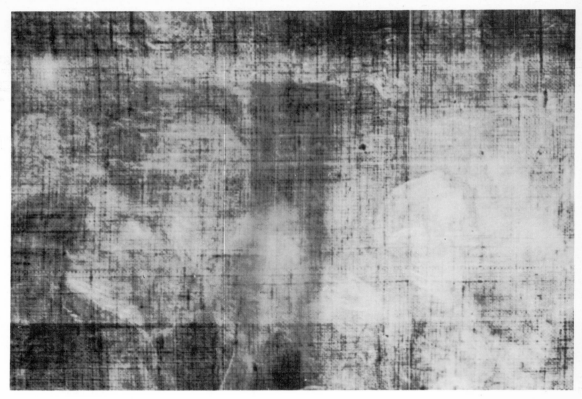

Plate 29 *The Tribuna* X-ray detail

1 *Gazzetta Toscana*, 24 August 1776. Sir John Dick (1720-1804), Baronet of Braid, British Consul at Leghorn, 1754-76. Robert Adam described him as 'a clever little man ... with a glib tongue, quick conception and good understanding, esteemed by all for his hospitality, genteel spirits and sweet behaviour'. He was nominated 'Chevalier' of the Order of St Anne on 25 March 1774 and received the insignia early in 1775.

2 *Correspondence of King George the Third*, ed. Sir J. Fortescue, vol. V (1928), p.50. In the Panshanger MSS. are two letters written from London, 17 June 1780 and (?late) in 1781, by Zoffany to Cowper about his attempts on Cowper's behalf to interest the King in the two pictures. The Earl's inventory of 1779, also with these MSS., includes both the *Madonnas* by Raphael that Cowper had acquired. I am very grateful to Mr. Francis Watson for lending me his calendar of the 3rd Earl Cowper's papers in these MSS. According to Farington (*Diary*, vol. VIII (1928), p.75, 5 June 1816), Zoffany had asked 5000 guineas from Cowper for the *Madonna*; Cowper offered him 500 guineas *plus* an annual pension of £100 for life which Zoffany received for 40 years. There is said to be documentary evidence of this in the Panshanger MSS.

3 Payments for the year 10 October 1763 – 10 October 1764 include payments to Stephen Slaughter, Surveyor of the King's Pictures, of expenses involved

his gaze is still on the *Satyr* [50]. More important: the cherubic Lord Plymouth [3] had to be moved a pace or two backwards. X-ray [Plate 29] shows him in his first position, his head almost exactly under that of the Infant Christ in the '*Niccolini-Cowper*' *Madonna*. At some stage Sir John Dick [2] was introduced into this little circle; he gazes down at the Madonna and is wearing the insignia of the Russian Order of St Anne of Schleswig-Holstein which he first wore in public at the christening of Lord Cowper's heir on 23 August 1776.[1] It seems, incidentally, as if the figure of Zoffany with his *Madonna* was painted in behind Lord Lewisham and Mr Stevenson; in other words, they were not apparently painted over it, although the transaction had surely taken place before they arrived in Florence.

There was perhaps a special purpose in Zoffany's and Lord Cowper's minds when it was decided to display the newly-bought Raphael in the context of the Tribuna. Cowper was passionately anxious to become a Knight of the Garter. He ingratiated himself with George III by sending him works of art from Italy. On 23 April 1780 he wrote to the king from Florence, offering him the *Madonna* and a *Self-portrait* of Raphael for £2500: 'Zoffany can inform your Majesty of them, as he has had them in his hands'.[2] The king did not, unfortunately, accept this offer and the Earl never got the Garter. It may be fanciful to imagine Zoffany prompting Lord Cowper to offer his new *Madonna* to the king; but Zoffany would have remembered the king's superb Raphael drawings at Buckingham House; he could have told Cowper of the moment, late in 1763 or early in 1764, when the Raphael Cartoons were bought up from Hampton Court to hang in the Saloon at Buckingham House;[3] and they may have thought to tempt the king by displaying, among the finest collection of Raphaels in Europe, a *Madonna* which the king could buy.

Finally there are the objects on the floor. In Mann's famous letter of 10 December 1779 to Walpole he records the approval of Zoffany's achievement and skill by 'our best judges here; but they found great fault in the perspective which, they say, is all wrong. I know that he was sensible of it himself, and tried to get assistance to correct it; but it was found

Plate 30 *The Tribuna* X-ray detail

impossible, and he carried it away as it was'.[1] He seems to have found, for example, that he could not draw or paint accurately, and in correct perspective, Buontalenti's very elaborately patterned floor. He certainly attempted it: the pattern can be seen with the naked eye, and more clearly in X-ray [Plate 30], running right through the foreground, except perhaps under the carpet on the right under Felton Hervey's chair. He probably covered some of the pattern with the mats in the foreground, in front of the group on the left and behind Sir Horace Mann. And it was possibly to cover up still more of the pattern that he introduced the apparently casual collection of works of art lying around the *Arrotino* [48] [Plate 31]. It is, indeed, possible that the *Arrotino* itself was put in at this stage: the base on which stands the *Cupid and Psyche* [49] was painted at first completely visible and the lowest part of it was only later concealed by the pieces in front of it. Behind the *Arrotino* are a large Apulian

in 'removing the Cartoons from Hampton Court Palace to the Queen's House in St. James's Park' (P.R.O., A.O.I., 420, 201).

1 Dr. Doran, op. cit., vol. II, pp.358-9.

Plate 31 *The Tribuna* detail

cratere [54] of the 4th century B.C. and an Etruscan helmet [55]; beyond the *Arrotino* are the famous Etruscan bronze Chimera [56], a Greek torso in bronze [61] and the Egyptian Ptahmose [60] of the eighteenth dynasty. In the foreground are three Roman *lucernae* [57, 58, 59]; the silver shield of the Consul Flavius Ardaburius Aspar [63], recently bought by the Grand Duke and here resting on a bronze head of Antinous [64]; a bust of Julius Caesar [62]; a South Italian *cratere* [65]; an Etruscan jug [66]; and a South Italian *situla* [67].[1] Zoffany paints these objects with his usual unflagging accuracy; and, as he had done when painting the *Hercules* [51], records damages (for example to the Chimera, the torso and the Egyptian figure), some of which have since been made good.

The presence of Etruscan objects in this miscellany in the foreground is a reminder of keen contemporary interest in Etruria: of the controversies in learned circles over the inter-relation of Greek, Roman and Etruscan influences, and of the discovery and acquisition of

1 I am very grateful to Dr. D. E. Strong for his help in identifying these pieces.

Plate 32 Johann Zoffany *Self-Portrait* Oil on canvas Uffizi Gallery, Florence

large deposits of Etruscan remains.[1] And although the scope and entirely arbitrary presence of the miscellany in the Tribuna would have offended the susceptibilities of Antonio Gori, who was so anxious that the Grand Duke's possessions should be arranged in a more archaeologically rational order, the scope of the anthology that Zoffany composes in *his* Tribuna is widened by this device to include examples of Egyptian, Etruscan, Greek and Roman, as well as renaissance and early baroque, art. Finally, and perhaps as a last tribute to the Grand Duke's good taste, he added to his assemblage on the floor the *Samian Sibyl* by Guercino [46] which Pietro Leopoldo had acquired early in 1777 from the estate of Alberigo Albergotti.[2]

At last, in April 1778, Zoffany left Florence.[3] He travelled to Parma, where he painted portraits of the reigning family: the Duchess, Maria Amalia, was a sister of the Grand Duke of Tuscany.[4] He left behind in Florence, for the Grand Duke's collection of self-portraits, the *Self-portrait* [Plate 32] which he had probably painted just before his departure: a polished, highly-finished performance, strangely unpleasant in expression. In the background and in the artist's hands are conventional reminders that Art is long while Life is short and in the picture behind him is an equally conventional warning of the temptations that can assail it and make it even shorter. In Parma he painted, on the other side of a very unsuccessful pastiche of Correggio [Plate 33], a less equivocal *Self-portrait* [Plate 34].[5] Disillusioned, weary and dishevelled, Zoffany has turned his back on his brush and palette and is putting on the habit of a Franciscan monk, but he joins the fraternity of Medmenham and not of Assisi. On a shelf above him he has placed a pack of cards, a bottle of wine and

1 For the controversy, see especially R. Wittkower, 'Piranesi's "Parere sul' Architettura"', *Journal of the Warburg Institute*, vol. II (1938–9), pp.147–58. The Grand Duke was particularly interested in the Chimera, which had been found near Arezzo in 1554 and had stood in the Palazzo Vecchio until 1717; and he had made a number of important archaeological purchases, especially, in 1768, of the 'museo della Casa *Galluzzi di Volterra*, nel quale era state riunita una ricca serie di urne, o cassette sepolcrali di alabastro, e di tupo con bassirilievi, e di vasi antichi a vernice nera, e di terra leggierissima, molti ornamenti muliebri d' oro assai singolari, gemme intagliate, bronzi, ed altre cose, il tutto disotterrato nei sepolcretti etruschi di quel territorio, e con questa nuova collezione di monumenti dei nostri antichi si accrebbe assai la raccolta che già stava riposta nella Galleria' (G. Bencivenni, *Saggio Istorico*, op. cit., vol. I, pp.70, 412–13).

2 The *Gazzetta Toscana* for 22 February 1777 devoted an enthusiastic notice to the purchase of this 'superbo quadro originale...Questo pezzo veramente singolare, non poteva esser meglio collocato che nel luogo ove per gloria della Città nostra stanno in deposito le produzioni più belle delle Arti tutte tanto antiche, ché moderne'.

3 See Appendix B, V. The *Gazzetta Toscana* records his departure on 6 June, although the number (it is no. 23 of the year 1778) is printed as April.

4 A. Ghidiglia Quantavalle, 'Il Pittore Johann Zoffany alla Corte di Don Ferdinando', *Aurea Parma*, Anno XXXIX, Fasc. I, Gennaio–Marzo 1955 (Parma).

5 It is stated to be inscribed *Cav. J. Zoffani. s Parma 1779 il 13 Marzo*. In the 1784 inventory of the Uffizi

Plate 33 Johann Zoffany *The Madonna and Child with St. Joseph* Oil on panel 17 × 15½ inches Palazzo della Pilotta, Parma

Plate 34 Johann Zoffany *Self-Portrait* Oil on panel

the *Self-portrait* given to the Grand Duke is in vol. I, f.275. Zoffany clearly painted a number of *Self-portraits* in Florence. On 20 January 1776 Maria Hadfield wrote to Humphry: 'Mr Zofani a finito il suo Ritratto e non restando contento, lui ne comincia un altro che sarà il terzo' (Original Correspondence, op. cit., vol. II, 41).

The *Gazzetta Toscana* for 6 November 1773 had reported that the Grand Duke had accepted from Zoffany 'una Madonna dipinta a posta sulla maniera antica dal sig. Giovanni Soffanj'; it had been presented to the Grand Duke by Zoffany at Poggio a Caiano and the Grand Duke had given him a 'superba tabacchiera d'oro smaltato a più colori di finissimo lavoro, e un richissimo anello di grossi brillanti'.

Plate 35 Pieter van Lint *The Medici Venus* Black chalk touched with white, and pen and grey wash on blue paper $16\frac{3}{8} \times 10\frac{5}{8}$ inches Metropolitan Museum of Art, New York Rogers Fund, 1964

a death's head: an association celebrated more wittily by Scythrop Glowry or Lord Byron. Under the shelf are a rosary, an engraving of the *Venus of Urbino* and frank reminders of the dangers of sacrificing to her too generously. In contrast with the gaiety of portraits in this vein by Knapton or Hogarth, there seems a calculated nastiness about this portrait. It echoes the disillusionment of an earlier artist, who had inscribed his drawing of Zoffany's other *Venus* [Plate 35]: 'Who loved me too much, lost health, wealth and soul'; and placed a death's head at her feet.

Zoffany returned to England as a member of the Academies of Bologna, Tuscany, Parma and Etruria and a Knight of the Holy Roman Empire. On 12 November 1779 Walpole was at last able to see the picture in Zoffany's house. Two days later he described it to Lady Upper Ossory as 'an astonishing piece of work with a vast deal of merit'.[1] But when he wrote to Mann (surely 'grown fat, jolly, young'), later in the day on which he had visited Zoffany, he was more critical. He was full of praise of Zoffany's representational skill, although he thought he had falsified the colours of the statues; but he considered the idea of the conversazione 'absurd . . . rendered more so by being crowded with a flock of travel-ling boys, and one does not know nor care whom. You and Sir John Dick, as Envoy and Consul, are very proper . . . Most of the rest are as impertinent as the names of church-wardens stuck up in parishes whenever a country church is repaired and whitewashed'.[2] Alas for Zoffany, the king and queen were equally shocked. What could they know or care about Loraine-Smith, Mr Doughty, the two Wilbrahams, Mr Watts, Mr Gordon or Valentine Knightley? As late as 1804 the king was still chafing at the impropriety of the whole thing: 'The King spoke of Zoffany's picture of the *Florentine Gallery* painted for him, & expressed wonder at Zoffany having done so improper a thing as to introduce the portraits of Sir Horace Man – Patch, & others. – He sd. the Queen wd. not suffer the picture to be placed in any of her apartments'.[3] By 23 August 1781 the picture was still on Zoffany's hands; and, although Walpole thought that it would 'rise in value, as a portrait of what that room *was*',[4] there was obviously considerable wrangling over the price Zoffany was to be paid for it, over and above the money he had received from the king or queen for his journey to and from Florence and for his expenses while he had been working there. Zoffany's widow appears to have stated that he was paid one thousand pounds for it;[5] but Zoffany may have expected at least double this sum. Mrs Papendiek tells the story of George III summoning the Royal Academicians to inspect the picture in a room at Kew Palace; they thought that it deserved an annual allowance of one thousand pounds for life and seven hundred pounds in immediate payment. It may have been at this point that Zoffany was accused of having lengthened his stay in Florence and accepted other commissions; Mrs Papendiek remained convinced that Zoffany received less than one thousand pounds for the picture. It was later stated that, on the advice of Benjamin West, the queen gave him six hundred guineas for it;[6] a contemporary source,[7] however, stated that in addition to fifteen hundred pounds paid out to cover Zoffany's expenses the king paid eight hundred pounds for the picture. Unfortunately, a fairly thorough search in official records has so far failed to find payments to Zoffany.

By 22 December 1788 the picture was at Kew, at last – perilously – in royal hands. 'During this day H.M𝑦. continued a little ticklish & He was obliged to be managed by The Attendants very attentively. He took a dislike to a Picture which hung in his room. It was the School of Florence by Zoffany. He had it immediately off the Nails on the Floor, before He was perceived to be busy with it. The Picture was directly moved into the Next room'.[8] Was it the pathetic, half-mad king in 1788 or a salacious visitor to an exhibition in Newcastle in 1888 who perpetrated the outrages on the *Venus of Urbino*?

Among much that I have had to omit in this Lecture are any observations upon the pic-

1 *Letters*, op. cit., vol. XI (1904), p.53.

2 Ibid., vol. XI, pp.48-49.

3 Joseph Farington, *Diary*, vol. III (1924), p.34, under 15 December 1804.

4 *Letters*, op. cit., vol. XII (1904), p.40.

5 Appendix A, II.

6 Mrs. Papendiek, op. cit., vol. I, pp.82-85; *The Literary Gazette*, 8 and 15 July 1826.

7 Quoted by Whitley, op. cit., vol. I, p.295.

8 *The Diaries of . . . Robert Fulke Greville*, ed. F. McKno Bladon (1930), p.130. Mann had confided to Walpole: 'I should think too the naked Venus which is the principal figure, will not please Her Majesty so much as it did the young men to whom it was shewed'.

ture's quality: upon Zoffany's crisp, fresh touch and gay, but never discordant, colour; upon the balance he maintains, remarkable in a work so long in the making; and upon the skilful concealment of the changes and modifications that we know he made from time to time. When the painting was cleaned in 1964 it was found to be in a very fine state; the removal of discoloured varnish revealed only slight losses of paint and all the gaiety and the sparkle of Zoffany's palette. Not that his Tribuna is to be judged solely as a work of art. Zoffany could not have painted, and Queen Charlotte might not have liked, Watteau's *L'Enseigne de Gersaint*. But professional judges in Florence and London thought highly of Zoffany's assiduity and skill. Bencivenni in Florence was, as we have seen, warm in praise of 'il genio, la capacità, e la diligenza . . . quella maestria, e verità' which Zoffany had lavished on the task. When the picture was shown at the Royal Academy in 1780 (68) as 'A room in the gallery of Florence, called the Tribuna, in which the principal part is calculated to show the different styles of the several masters', there were perceptive comments in the press: tributes to an 'amazing monument of imitative talents' and a 'striking instance of laborious industry'.[1] The writer in the *London Courant* for 4 May 1780, while admiring the accuracy of the copies and resemblances of the portraits was troubled by 'the *equal light*, which is diffused throughout the whole, and which perhaps was *necessary* to show each picture distinctly, and from the great number of persons painted in the room, the picture appears crowded and confused'. The *Morning Post*, too, on 6 May 1780, praised the skill with which Zoffany had imitated the different styles of the several masters, but thought the picture not void of imperfections: 'among which we may mention as the principal its want of keeping, and the necessary contrast of light and shade'. Zoffany would perhaps have been particularly gratified when he read the *Morning Chronicle*: 'this accurate picture has the same effect on the spectator which the gallery itself has on first entering it; the multitude of excellencies contained in it, dissipate our ideas, and it requires some time to arrange them before we can coolly examine the merit of any individual piece'.

From a mixture of indefatigable industry, cupidity, self-seeking and imagination, Zoffany had produced an astonishing work: a personal anthology from a great collection and an imaginary conversation-piece. By composing a hypothetical 'hang' in the Tribuna he had created a vivid impression of the original idea behind the creation of the room itself. The room had by now lost much of the atmosphere, exotic and fantastic, of a sixteenth-century *Wunder-kammer*, a sparkling shrine to set off the skills of the Florentine craftsmen and the splendours of the Florentine collections. The intelligence of the young Grand Duke had encouraged a more lucid and rational spirit throughout the Gallery. This is the phase in its history which Zoffany records. Nowadays the room is very different [Plate 36]: pierced by two more openings so that it can be thrown into the sequence of rooms on either side of it and hung with indifferent or pointless pictures. As early as 1794 we find Lord Palmerston, who had first seen the Gallery in 1763, writing in his diary: 'We found the Gallery much alterd the new director having changed ye Situation of most of the Pictures upon an Idea of arranging them according to the Schools'.[2]

But we perhaps value Zoffany's picture even more highly as a record of the Grand Tour, which has been the most powerful civilising influence in four centuries of life north of the Alps. Perhaps no tour of Italy, undertaken from England, was more carefully planned – certainly none was more fruitful – than that begun by Edward Gibbon in 1764. On 20 June 1764, soon after his arrival in Florence, he set out in a letter to his sister the varied aspects of the experience. Some of these were, of course, disagreeable: 'bad roads, and indifferent inns . . . and especially the continual converse one is obliged to have with the vilest part of mankind, Innkeepers, post masters, and custom house officers'; but a traveller was amply

1 *The Morning Chronicle*, 20 May 1780. The writer in *The Literary Gazette* for 15 July 1826 described the excitement of seeing the picture when it was shown at the British Institution and records certain traditions about it 'yet told . . . at the tables of a few remaining branches of the ancient *cognos*'. He alleges that Zoffany had charged twenty guineas a head for the privilege of being inserted into the picture and had on occasion rubbed a head out in order to gain a further twenty guineas by painting a later visitor over an earlier one.

2 MS. at Broadlands.

repaid for these 'little mortifications' by the wonders which filled his eye at every turn and 'have already made me pass some of the most entertaining days I have yet known'. We can still share the discomfort and the wonder; but only the rarest spirits are so fired by what they see in Italy as to add: 'I do not despair of being able one day to produce something by way of a Description of ancient Italy'.[1] If one could contemplate Zoffany's Tribuna and follow to their end the many enthralling lines of thought and research it suggests – if, to the plain account that I have tried to set out in this Lecture, one could add that 'tincture of philosophy and criticism' which Gibbon thought so essential in any historical under-taking – the picture itself might be found to have a little of the inspiring quality of the experience which it so notably illustrates.

1 *The Letters of Edward Gibbon*, ed. J. E. Norton (1956), vol. I, pp. 180-1.

Plate 36 The Tribuna of the Uffizi at the present day

Appendix A

Notes on Zoffany by Joseph Farington. The notes are contained in vols. II and IV of Farington's MS. Notebooks on artists, preserved in the Royal Library, Windsor Castle.

I   *Vol. IV, ff.41–43. At top of f.41 is written :* many particulars related by himself, Decr 18th 1795 to me.

1 *Note by Farington :* The German name is Züffall – *Zoffany is the Italian pronunciation. The gaps in the note are as Farington left them.*

2 *Corrected by Farington to :* near.

3 *An insertion by Farington.*

4 *Corrected from :* Elvon.

[f.41] **Johan Zoffany**[1]
was born at[2] Frankfort on the Mayne[3] a Town the Capital of [   ] belonging to the Prince of Baden,[3] March 13th, 1734. His Father was

    Indicating at an early age a talent for drawing, He was placed at Elwangen,[4] the principal town of the Bishoprick of that name, under [   ] to learn the elements of that art. From Elvon He was removed to Ratisbon to receive instructions from Mr Speare, an artist of merit, who had studied at Rome. Here He remained three years. In 1750 He went to Auxsbourgh, and determined to proceed to Rome. at that time a Coach went twice a year from Auxsbourgh to Rome, and each passenger paid twelve guineas for which all expences were included. By order of Zoffanys father a place was taken for him in this conveyance; but such was his desire to see the countries through which He had to pass, at leisure, that sending his baggage only, by the coach, He performed the whole journey on foot, and such was his enthusiastic desire to see Rome, as to cause him to walk on the day He entered that City 46 miles. During this pedestrian expedition [f.42] He made many drawings of Landscape scenery.

    Zoffany arrived at Rome, 1750, where He studied under Masucci, a Scholar of Carlo Maratt, about three years : after which He placed himself under Mengs, and remained with him Seven years; during which time He made excursions to Naples, Venice &c. – From Italy Zoffany returned to Ratisbon, and became painter to the Elector of Treves; for whom He executed several works in Fresco.[5] Here He remained three years.[5] From Ratis-

5 *An insertion by Farington.*

6 *Written above with carat.*

aged 26 bon He came to England[6] in 1760[6] and was engaged to paint draperies for Benjamin Wilson, but a disagreement between them having taken place, He soon quitted that employ, & painted some small whole lengths, which had so much merit as to draw to Him public attention. Mr Garrick became a great admirer of his art, and frequently sat to Him in various characters, & His reputation rose very high as a painter of conversation pieces.

aged 28   In the year 1762 He exhibited His picture of Mr Garrick in the Character of the Farmer returned from London; in 1763 Mr Garrick, & Mrs Cibber, in the characters of Jaffier & Belvidera; in 1765 Mr Foote, in the character of Major Sturgeon, in the Mayor of Garratt; and Mr Moody in the character of Foigard; in 1765 Mr Garrick, in the character of Sir John Brute, in the Drunken scene in the Provoked Wife; in 1766, Mr Garrick, in the character of Lord Chalkstone; in 1767, Mrs Beard, & Mr Shuter, in the characters of Hawthorne & Justice Woodcock[7] & Mr. Dunstall[7] in a scene in Love in a Village; which

7 *Written above with carat.*

picture was also exhibited in September 1768 in an Exhibition made to shew to the King of Denmark the state of the arts in this country. On the 10th of December 1768 the Royal Academy was established under His Majesty's patronage, and the first [*f.43*] Exhibition of the Royal Academicians was in the spring of 1769 but Mr Zoffany continued a Member of the Incorporated Society of Artists from those Artists who had now become Royal Academicians had seceded, – with the Incorporated Society Mr Zoffany in 1769 at their room in spring gardens, exhibited another Theatrical representation, a scene in "The Devil upon two Sticks", in which Mr Foote was introduced in the character of [   ] & Mr Weston in that of Dr Last. Soon after this period Mr Zoffany was induced to quit the Incorporated Society & to unite Himself with the Royal Academicians, and had the honor of being added to that Body, not by *Election*, but was *nominated by the King*. Mr Zoffany had been a very popular Exhibitor, and the Academicians were sensible that it would much contribute to decide the superiority in their favor in an ensuing Exhibition, which at that time they could scarcely boast of, as many able Artists continued members of the Incorporated Society. Those Artists who formed the Body of Academicians at the Institution of the Royal Academy were nominated by the King, but it was established that all future Vacancies should be filled by *Election*. To this, however, Mr Zoffany wd not submit; He would not place Himself at the option of the members of the Academy, therefore to obtain Him, it was proposed to the King to place him on a footing with the original members by nominating Him a Royal Academician. – At the 2d Exhibition of the Royal Academy in

aged 36 1770 Mr Zoffany proved Himself entitled to the Honor which had been bestowed upon him, by Exhibiting a picture, "The Last Scene in the Alchymist" in which Mr Garrick was represented in the character of Abel Drugger, with Bensley, & Packer in [   ]. This, perhaps, may be considered His Chef D'ouvre of Theatrical representations. It excited the highest degree of admiration, and was bought by Sir Joshua Reynolds for 100 guineas, at the particular request of the Earl of Carlisle, Sir Joshua sold it to Him for 120 guineas, and gave the difference to the Royal Academy Fund.

II   *Inserted in vol. IV of Farington's MS. notebooks is the following later account, numbered IV 41 (A), which is a loose sheet.*
This account of Zoffany was given by Mrs Zoffany, His widow, to Miss Green, neice to George Dance R.A. in July or August 1811. —

Johan Zoffanij R.A.
was born at Frankfort on the Mayne in the year 1733.

His Father was Architect to the Prince of Tours & Taxis. He was brought up & educated with the son of that Prince till the age of thirteen, when He felt so great a passion for painting (of which He had at that time given many specimens) that He ran away from his freinds, in order to study at Rome and to devote Himself to that art. upon His Fathers discovery of His intentions He obtained a recommendation to one of the Cardinals, by whom He was patronised, and placed under the care of the Convent of Buon Fratelli.

He resided near twelve years in Italy improving himself in His profession, and visited most of the principal cities there. He returned to Germany for a short time, from whence He came over to England in the year 1758.

He painted a picture of Garrick in "The Farmer's return" which attracted the attention of Lord Bute, who warmly patronised Him, and introduced Him to the notice of the Royal Family.

In the year 17[ ] He entered into an engagement with Sir Joseph Bankes, Dr Solander, & Dr Lind, to accompany Captain Cook round the world, and had even sent everything on board for that purpose; but finding himself disappointed in His accommodation for painting, He declined going upon this enterprising expedition. Being, however, in an unsettled state, having given up his house & business, and displeased many of his patrons by leaving their pictures in an unfinished state, He determined to revisit Italy. Upon declaring this intention to Her Majesty, she patronised Him, and procured him letters of introduction to the principal persons there, with a present of £300 for His Journey, and an order to paint for Her, the Florence Gallery, which He executed & rec.^d for it a thousand pounds.

He left England in 1772 and remained on the Continent seven years. He painted a picture of the Grand Duke & Duchess of Tuscany & their family, by order of Maria Theresa, Empress of Germany, who was also one of His great patronesses, and in 1777 He took a journey to Vienna to present this picture himself to the Empress, who handsomely rewarded him & created him a Baron of that Empire. During this residence in Italy He was elected member of the Academies of Bologna, Tuscany, Parma & Etrusca.

In 1779 He returned to England & continued to follow His profession.

In 1783 He took a sudden determination to go to India, where He made a considerable fortune by His paintings & drawings, and travelled for His pleasure far into the Country. In 1790 He returned to His family in England & continued painting for many years.

He was twice married; first in Germany to a native of that Country, & secondly in England to Mary Thomas by whom He left four daughters.

He was one of the original members of the Royal Academy.

He died the 11th of November 1810 at Strand on the Green, & was buried at Kew, aged 77.

III   *Inserted in vol. IV of Farington's MS. notebooks is a sheet of rough notes, numbered IV 41 (B), on the back of a letter (of no date) from Farington to Samuel Lysons. The notes are apparently part of a draft for section I above. The details, however, of Zoffany's Italian period are slightly different from those in Section II above.*

. . . In 1772 went to Florence was in Italy 7 yeares cheifly at F. & at Parma & to England in 1780.

at Florence – painted for the Empress The family of Tuscany 10 figures large as life. – At Parma the parmesan family Duke & Duchess ½ lengths, 3 children whole length, –) Florentine gallery for Queen of England, – went to Vienna from Florence to finish Florentine picture 1775 painted old Empress whole length – made Baron of Empire, – free of expense 300 ducats, –

IV   *Vol. II, f.61*

Zouffoli, (Zoffany)

His Father was an Hungarian a Lieutenant of Hussars – His Mother from[1] Ratisbon – she followed the army – Her Husband killed in the neighborond of Belgrade in war with Turkey – returned to Ratisbon – bound Zoffany to a Painter there.

related by Wickstead His Pupil to Fuseli who communicated it to me in Novr 1804.

---

1 *Altered from :* a native of .

Appendix B

Documents, relating to Zoffany's work in the Gallery, preserved in the Public Record Office and in the Archivio degli Uffizi.

I   *Archivio degli Uffizi, Filza V (1772), 26. Letter from Angelo Tavanti, a member of the Council of Finances, to the Director of the Gallery, 13 August 1772.*

Illmo Sigre: Sigre: ProeClmo

     Avendo S.A.R. accordato al Pittore Zoffany Inglese di dipingere del vero La veduta della Tribuna della Re Galleria per dover Servire una tal veduta per S.M. La Regina d'Inghilterra; ne rendo intesa VS. Illma affinche in conformità di tal permissione venga dato il commodo al detto Pittore di fare L'operazione Suddetta con quelle assistenze, e cautele che giudicherà opportune.

E con perfetta Stima mi confermo
Di VS. Illma
Dalla Segrie: delle Ri Finze
Li 13: Agosto 1772.

_____

Devotmo ed oblmo servre
Angelo Tavanti

Eseguito
Sigre: Direttre: della
Re: Galleria

Illmo Sigre: Sigre: Prone Clmo
In replica al compitissimo Biglietto di VS. Illma degl' 11 : Ste: hò L'onore di Significarle che Sono Stati dati gli ordini opportuni al Dirette: della Re: Galleria perche dia il comodo al Sigre: Zoffany di dipingere dal vero La veduta della Tribuna di detta Galleria, a forma della permissione concessane da S.A.R.

E col piu distinto Ossequio mi confermo.
Di VS. Illma
Dalla Segreta: dlle Ri: Finze:
li 13 : Agosto 1772 :

Sigre: Cave: Orazio Mann

Devotmo ed ossmo servre
Angelo Tavanti

All' Illmo Sigre: Cavre: Orazio Mann rassegna il Suo rispetto Angelo Tavanti, ed hà l'onore di Significargli che Sono Stati dati gli Ordini opportuni perchè Sia permesso al Sigr Foy di modellare in creta il Bacco di Michel'angelo esistente in Galleria, ma non ha potuto Servire Sua Sigria:Illma rispetto all'Apollo, essendo questo collocato nella Stanza detta La Tribuna, in cui per diversi riflessi non pùo permettersi di fare La modellatura di detta Statua, e si conferma
Devmo: ed Obbmo: Servitore . . .
Li 28 : Aple 1772

IV   *Archivio degli Uffizi, Filza VI (1773), 33. Memorandum submitted to the Grand Duke of Tuscany by Raimondo Cocchi, custodian of the medals and gems in the Gallery, attaching a petition from Vincenzo Spampani.*

Altezza Reale

R. 30 Ap̄le 1773

  Vincenzo Spampani, Umilissimo Servo, e suddito della R.A.V. devotamente la supplica voler le permettere di poter disegnare Le statue della R. Galleria che della grazie quam Deus.

  Io Vincenzo Spampani mano propria.

Altezza Reale

  E' Stato Sempre concesso disegnar Le Statue del Corridore, Per quelle della Tribuna bisognerebbe tenervi uno in guardia Come fanno al Pittor Zoffanj, E ciò perché così comanda V.A.R. nel suo R̥ Motu proprio de 7. Marzo. Già si studia sui gessi meglio che sulle Statue, per amor dei falsi lumi e delle macchie della patina; E delle buone di Galleria ci Sono i gessi qua è Là; Forse L'esser visti disegnare in publico e dai forestieri, puo' giovare ai giovani, e per questo Lo Spampani avrà chiesto E per il Corridore in tal Caso crederei che gli basterà. E prostr° baccio La Real Veste.

> Di Vostra Altezza Reale
> 2. Maggio 1773.
> Umilissimo Obb^mo: Suddittoe
> Servitore Raimondo Cocchi

V   *Archivio degli Uffizi, Filza V (1772), with item 26 (see no. I above).*

Quadri dipinti dal Cav̥ Gio. Zoffany nel suo

Quadro della Tribuna[1]

Questo Quadro deve fare il compagno al uno fatto dal cav̥̥ Zoffany con La Veduta dell'Accademia di Londra che va in Stampa

Venere di Tiziano in terra fra Le mani del Bastianelli [47]

Venere di Lodovico caracci [23]

Carità di Guido ne Pitti [24]

Madonna di Tiziano [29]

S. Gio. Bāt̄ta di raffaello [30]

Madonna di Guido [31]

Cleopatra ne Pitti [38]

Famiglia di Rubens ne Pitti [39]

Leon X. [?pure] ne Pitti [40]

1 I have added in square brackets after each painting its appropriate number on the Key.

Madonna della Leggiola ne Pitti [25]
Madonna del correggio [26]
ritratto del Galileo di Giusto [27]
Madonna dell'Uccellino di raffaello [32]
Altra [34]
Abramo con Agar di Pietro di Cortona [41]
Cristo della Moneta del caravaggio [42]
Giuliano del Bronzino de' Pitti [43]
Due ritratti di Albens [35, 36]
Madonna di Pietro Perugino della camera degli Stipi [37]
Sibilla del Guercino posta in terra [46]
Marte e Venere di Rubens de Pitti [33]

Vi sono alcune delle Statue della Tribuna
vari pezzi di antichità in Bronzo [?pure] con
molti ritratti di Persone cognite in atto
di osservare La med.ª: fra quali il Sud.º p.mº custode
vi era il can. Querci ma doppo La morte fu Levato

La Madonna del Parmigianino

Una Madonna col Figlio di raffaello coll'anno
MDVIII. (altri leggono XVIII.) di Milord Cowper [45]

Il cav.ᵉ Zoffany e partito per portare il suo
Quadro nell'Aprile 1778

VI *P.R.O., S.P. 105/321,219. Letter from Tavanti to Mann, 27 August 1772.*
Angelo Tavanti risegna il Suo distinto ossequio all' Ill.mºSig.rᵉ Cav.rᵉ Mann, e in replica al suo pregiat.mº Biglietto de' 21 del cadente si trova col dispiacere di significargli, che non può accordarsi al Pittore Sig. Barren la permissione di copiare la Venere di Tiziano esistente nella Real Galleria, essendo questa stata anche negata recentemente per giusti riflessi.

E si conferma Devot.mº ed Obb.mº Servitore.
Di Seg.riª delle R.li Finanze 27. Agosto 1772.

Index